THESE 6 STACKING TOYS WILL KEEP LITTLE ONES (and maybe few not so little ones!) OCCUPIED FOR HOURS.

The stacking actions promote eye-hand coordination; the colors and characters can also be used as learning tools. Single crochet stitches, combined with colorful medium weight yarns, create thick durable shapes that are then stuffed and stacked. I've given basic stand and ring patterns, along with 6 fun and whimsical themes to dress up the stand and rings. Buzzy bees, tasty doughnuts, a colorful rainbow, pretty flowers, safari animals, and a cute octopus (along with her starfish BFFs) are just waiting to entertain and delight.

Basic Patterns	2	All Hands on Deck	32
So Cute Safari!	6	Sunny Rainbow	38
Its the Bees!	16	General Instructions	42
Sprinkled Donuts	22	Yarn Information	46
Tower of Flowers	28	Meet Tammy Ramsey	48

LEISURE ARTS, INC.
Maumelle, Arkansas

basic Patterns

STITCH GUIDE

SINGLE CROCHET 2 TOGETHER
(abbreviated sc2tog)

Pull up a loop in each of next 2 sc, YO and draw through all 3 loops on hook **(counts as one sc)**.

BASIC STAND

Rnd 1 (Right side)**:** With color indicated, make an adjustable loop to form a ring ***(Figs. 1a-d, page 43)***; work 8 sc in ring; do **not** join, place a marker to indicate the beginning of the rnd ***(see Markers, page 44)***.

Note: Loop a short piece of yarn around any stitch to mark Rnd 1 as **right** side.

Rnd 2: 2 Sc in each sc around: 16 sc.

Rnd 3: (Sc in next sc, 2 sc in next sc) around: 24 sc.

Rnd 4: (Sc in next 2 sc, 2 sc in next sc) around: 32 sc.

Rnd 5: (Sc in next 3 sc, 2 sc in next sc) around: 40 sc.

Rnd 6: (Sc in next 4 sc, 2 sc in next sc) around: 48 sc.

Rnd 7: (Sc in next 5 sc, 2 sc in next sc) around: 56 sc.

Rnd 8: (Sc in next 6 sc, 2 sc in next sc) around: 64 sc.

Rnd 9: (Sc in next 7 sc, 2 sc in next sc) around: 72 sc.

Rnd 10: (Sc in next 8 sc, 2 sc in next sc) around: 80 sc.

Rnd 11: (Sc in next 9 sc, 2 sc in next sc) around: 88 sc.

Rnd 12: (Sc in next 10 sc, 2 sc in next sc) around: 96 sc.

Rnd 13: Sc in each sc around.

Rnd 14: (Sc in next 11 sc, 2 sc in next sc) around: 104 sc.

Rnd 15: (Sc in next 12 sc, 2 sc in next sc) around: 112 sc.

Rnd 16: (Sc in next 13 sc, 2 sc in next sc) around: 120 sc.

Using the crocheted circle as a pattern, trim plastic canvas circle slightly larger than the crocheted piece; set piece aside.

Rnd 17: (Sc in next 13 sc, sc2tog) around: 112 sc.

Rnd 18: (Sc in next 12 sc, sc2tog) around: 104 sc.

Rnd 19: (Sc in next 11 sc, sc2tog) around: 96 sc.

Rnd 20: (Sc in next 10 sc, sc2tog) around: 88 sc.

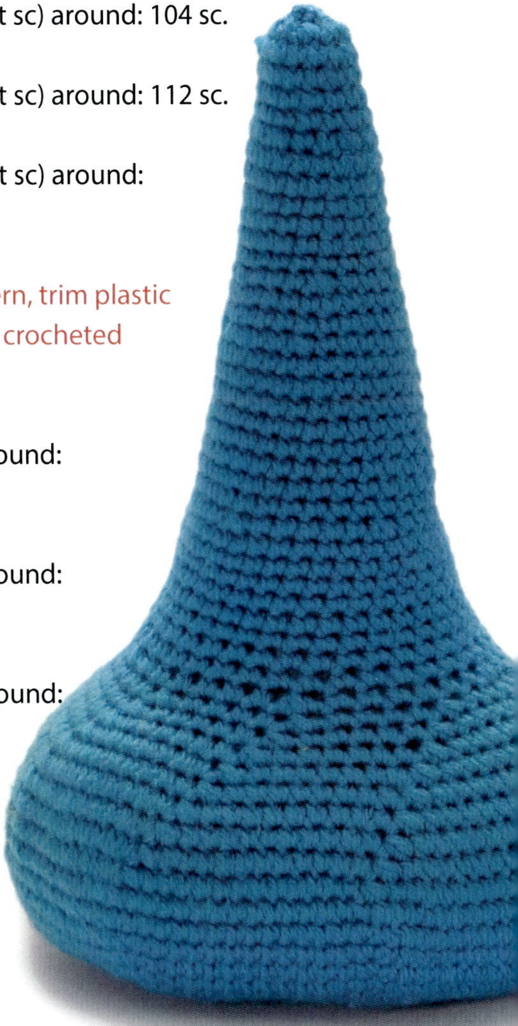

Insert plastic canvas circle inside crocheted piece to form the bottom of the stand.

Rnd 21: (Sc in next 9 sc, sc2tog) around: 80 sc.

Rnd 22: (Sc in next 8 sc, sc2tog) around: 72 sc.

Rnd 23: (Sc in next 7 sc, sc2tog) around: 64 sc.

Rnd 24: (Sc in next 6 sc, sc2tog) around: 56 sc.

Rnd 25: (Sc in next 5 sc, sc2tog) around: 48 sc.

Rnd 26: (Sc in next 4 sc, sc2tog) around: 40 sc.

Rnd 27: (Sc in next 6 sc, sc2tog) around: 35 sc.

Rnds 28-35: Sc in each sc around.

Stuff piece firmly with polyester fiberfill.

Rnd 36: (Sc in next 5 sc, sc2tog) around: 30 sc.

Rnds 37-44: Sc in each sc around.

Add polyester fiberfill as you continue to work.

Rnd 45: (Sc in next 4 sc, sc2tog) around: 25 sc.

Rnds 46 and 47: Sc in each sc around.

Rnd 48: (Sc in next 3 sc, sc2tog) around: 20 sc.

Rnds 49-54: Sc in each sc around.

Rnd 55: (Sc in next 2 sc, sc2tog) around: 15 sc.

Rnds 56-59: Sc in each sc around.

Rnd 60: Sc2tog around until only 5 sts remain; slip st in next sc, finish off leaving a long end for sewing.

Weave yarn end through the sts on the last rnd to close ***(Fig. 4, page 44)***; secure end.

BASIC RINGS

Ring lengths may need to be adjusted depending on your stitch tension. Looser stitches will stretch more when stuffed so you may need to decrease the number of rounds. You may measure the ring around the stand before finishing and add just the number of rounds as needed.

Bottom Ring

Rnd 1 (Right side)**:** With color indicated, make an adjustable loop to form a ring; work 6 sc in ring; do **not** join, place a marker to indicate the beginning of the rnd.

Rnd 2: 2 Sc in each sc around: 12 sc.

Rnd 3: (Sc in next sc, 2 sc in next sc) around: 18 sc.

Rnd 4: Sc in each sc around.

Repeat Rnd 4 for a total of 70 rnds, stuffing the tube firmly approximately every 10 rnds; slip st in next sc, finish off leaving a long end for sewing.

Sew the tube to itself to form a ring.

Second Ring

Work same as bottom ring for a total of 60 rnds.

Third Ring

Work same as bottom ring for a total of 50 rnds.

Top Ring

Work same as bottom ring for a total of 40 rnds.

so cute Safari!

Finished Height: Approximately 8½" (21.5 cm)

EASY

SHOPPING LIST

Yarn (Medium Weight)

- ☐ Green - 165 yards (151 meters)
- ☐ Teal - 75 yards (68.5 meters)
- ☐ Blue - 55 yards (50.5 meters)
- ☐ Gold - 50 yards (45.5 meters)
- ☐ Dk Brown - 45 yards (41 meters)
- ☐ Lt Grey - 10 yards (9 meters)
- ☐ Lt Blue - 10 yards (9 meters)
- ☐ Dk Yellow - 10 yards (9 meters)
- ☐ Tan - 10 yards (9 meters)
- ☐ Orange - 10 yards (9 meters)
- ☐ White - small amount

Crochet Hook

- ☐ Size E (3.5 mm)

Additional Supplies

- ☐ 9½" (24 cm) Plastic canvas circle
- ☐ Polyester fiberfill
- ☐ Embroidery floss (for features) - Black and White
- ☐ Tapestry needle
- ☐ Yarn needle

GAUGE INFORMATION

Gauge is **not** of great importance as long as your crochet fabric is very dense *(see Gauge, page 43)*.

STAND

With Green, work Basic Stand, page 2.

RINGS

Bottom Ring

With Teal, work same as Basic Bottom Ring, page 5.

HEAD

Rnd 1 (Right side)**:** With Teal, make an adjustable loop to form a ring; work 6 sc in ring; do **not** join, place a marker to indicate the beginning of the rnd.

Note: Mark Rnd 1 as **right** side.

Rnd 2: 2 Sc in each sc around: 12 sc.

Rnd 3: (Sc in next sc, 2 sc in next sc) around: 18 sc.

Rnd 4: (Sc in next 2 sc, 2 sc in next sc) around: 24 sc.

Rnds 5-7: Sc in each sc around.

Rnd 8: (Sc in next 2 sc, sc2tog) around: 18 sc.

Rnd 9: (Sc in next sc, sc2tog) around: 12 sc.

Stuff piece with polyester fiberfill.

Rnd 10: Sc2tog around; slip st in next sc, finish off leaving a long end for sewing.

Sew the Head to the ring at joining so that it sits slightly raised.

FOOT (Make 4)

Rnd 1 (Right side)**:** With Lt Grey, make an adjustable loop to form a ring; work 6 sc in ring; do **not** join, place a marker to indicate the beginning of the rnd.

Note: Mark Rnd 1 as **right** side.

Rnd 2: 2 Sc in each sc around changing to Teal in last sc made ***(Fig. 3, page 44)***; cut Lt Grey: 12 sc.

Rnds 3-6: Sc in each sc around; at end of Rnd 6, slip st in next sc, finish off leaving a long end for sewing.

Sew Feet evenly spaced around ring.

TRUNK

Rnd 1 (Right side)**:** With Lt Grey, make an adjustable loop to form a ring; work 6 sc in ring changing to Teal in last sc made; cut Lt Grey, do **not** join, place a marker to indicate the beginning of the rnd.

Note: Mark Rnd 1 as **right** side.

Rnds 2-5: Sc in each sc around.

Rnd 6: (Sc in next sc, 2 sc in next sc) around: 9 sc.

Rnd 7: (Sc in next 2 sc, 2 sc in next sc) around: 12 sc.

Rnd 8: (Sc in next 3 sc, 2 sc in next sc) around: 15 sc.

Rnd 9: (Sc in next 4 sc, 2 sc in next sc) around: 18 sc.

Rnd 10: Sc in each sc around; slip st in next sc, finish off leaving a long end for sewing.

With long end, stitch down from slip st to tip of Trunk and then back up to edge of Rnd 10. Pull tight to force tip to curl up. Knot yarn to side of trunk to hold curled shape.

EAR (Make 2)

Inner

Rnd 1 (Right side)**:** With Lt Grey, make an adjustable loop to form a ring; work 6 sc in ring; do **not** join, place a marker to indicate the beginning of the rnd.

Note: Mark Rnd 1 as **right** side.

Rnd 2: 2 Sc in each sc around: 12 sc.

Rnd 3: (Sc in next sc, 2 sc in next sc) around; slip st in next sc, finish off leaving a long end for sewing: 18 sts.

Outer

Rnd 1 (Right side)**:** With Teal, make an adjustable loop to form a ring; work 6 sc in ring; do **not** join, place a marker to indicate the beginning of the rnd.

Note: Mark Rnd 1 as **right** side.

Rnd 2: 2 Sc in each sc around: 12 sc.

Rnd 3: (Sc in next sc, 2 sc in next sc) around: 18 sc.

Rnd 4: (Sc in next 2 sc, 2 sc in next sc) around; slip st in next sc, finish off: 24 sts.

With **wrong** sides together and using long end, sew Inner and Outer Ear together.

Tail: Holding 2 strands **each** of Teal and Lt Grey together, ch 4; finish off.
Trim strands at one end to ½" (12 mm).

Using photo as a guide for placement, page 8:

- Sew Trunk to Head, stuffing lightly.
- Sew Ears to each side of Head
- Sew Tail to back of ring
- With Black embroidery floss, add satin stitch eyes ***(Figs. 6a & b, page 45)***.

Second Ring

With Blue, work same as Basic Second Ring.

HEAD
With Blue, work same as Bottom Ring Head, page 9.

FOOT (Make 4)
Work same as Bottom Ring Foot, using Lt Blue for Rnds 1 and 2 and Blue for the remainder of the Foot.

SNOUT
Rnd 1 (Right side)**:** With Lt Blue, ch 8; sc in second ch from hook and in next 5 chs, 3 sc in last ch; working in free loops on opposite side of ch ***(Fig. 2, page 44)***, sc in next 6 chs, 3 sc in next ch; do **not** join, place a marker to indicate the beginning of the rnd: 18 sc.

Note: Mark Rnd 1 as **right** side.

Rnds 2 and 3: Sc in each sc around; at end of Rnd 3, slip st in next sc, finish off leaving a long end for sewing.

EAR (Make 2)
Rnd 1 (Right side)**:** With Blue, make an adjustable loop to form a ring; work 6 sc in ring; do **not** join, finish off leaving a long end for sewing.

Tail: With Blue, ch 4; sc in second ch from hook and in last 2 chs; finish off leaving a long end for sewing.

Using photo as a guide for placement:

- Sew Snout to Head, stuffing lightly.
- Sew Ears to each side of Head.
- Sew Tail to back of ring.
- With Black embroidery floss, add satin stitch eyes and straight stitch nostrils *(Fig. 5, page 45)*.
- With White yarn, add vertical tooth at each side of Snout.

Third Ring

With Gold, work same as Basic Third Ring.

HEAD

With Gold, work same as Bottom Ring Head.

FOOT (Make 4)

Work same as Bottom Ring Foot, using Dk Yellow for Rnds 1 and 2 and Gold for the remainder of the Foot.

CHEEK (Make 2)

Rnd 1 (Right side)**:** With Dk Yellow, make an adjustable loop to form a ring; work 6 sc in ring; do **not** join, place a marker to indicate the beginning of the rnd.

Note: Mark Rnd 1 as **right** side.

Rnd 2: 2 Sc in each sc around; slip st in next sc, finish off leaving a long end for sewing.

EAR (Make 2)

Row 1 (Right side)**:** With Dk Yellow, ch 4; sc in second ch from hook and in last 2 chs: 3 sc.

Note: Mark Row 1 as **right** side.

Row 2: Turn; skip first sc, sc in last 2 sc: 2 sc.

Row 3: Turn; skip first sc, slip st in last sc; finish off leaving long end for sewing.

MANE

With Orange, ch 25; sc in second ch from hook, 3 dc in next ch, (sc in next ch, 3 dc in next ch) across; finish off leaving a long end for sewing.

Tail: Holding 2 strands **each** of Gold and Dk Yellow together, ch 4; finish off.

Trim strands at one end to ½" (12 mm).

Using photo as a guide for placement, page 12:

- Sew Cheeks to Head, stuffing lightly.
- Sew Ears to top of Head.
- Sew Mane around Head (in front of Ears).
- Sew Tail to back of ring.
- With Black embroidery floss, add satin stitch nose, a straight stitch vertical line between Cheeks, and straight stitch eyes.
- With White embroidery floss, add straight stitch whiskers.

Top Ring

With Dk Brown, work same as Basic Top Ring.

HEAD

With Dk Brown, work same as Bottom Ring Head.

FOOT (Make 4)

Work same as Bottom Ring Foot, using Tan for Rnds 1 and 2 and Dk Brown for remainder of Foot.

FACE

Rnd 1 (Right side)**:** With Tan, make an adjustable loop to form a ring; work 6 sc in ring; do **not** join, place a marker to indicated the beginning of the rnd.

Note: Mark Rnd 1 as **right** side.

Rnd 2: 2 Sc in each sc around: 12 sc.

Rnd 3: (Sc in next sc, 2 sc in next sc) around; slip st in next sc, finish off leaving a long end for sewing: 18 sts.

SNOUT

Rnd 1 (Right side)**:** With Tan, ch 6; sc in second ch from hook and in next 3 chs, 3 sc in last ch; working in free loops on opposite side of ch, sc in next 4 chs, 3 sc in next ch; do **not** join, place a marker to indicate the beginning of the rnd: 14 sc.

Note: Mark Rnd 1 as **right** side.

Rnd 2: Sc in each sc around; slip st in next sc, finish off leaving a long end for sewing.

EAR (Make 2)

Rnd 1 (Right side)**:** With Dk Brown, make an adjustable loop to form a ring; work 8 sc in ring; join with slip st to first sc, finish off leaving a long end for sewing.

Tail: With Dk Brown, ch 18; sc in second ch from hook and in each ch across; finish off leaving a long end for sewing.

Using photo as a guide for placement:

- Sew Face to Head.
- Sew Snout to Head, stuffing lightly.
- Sew Ears to each side of Head.
- Sew Tail to back of ring.
- With Black embroidery floss, add satin stitch eyes and straight stitch nostrils and a mouth.

it's the Bees!

Finished Height: Approximately 9¾" (25 cm)

EASY

SHOPPING LIST

Yarn (Medium Weight)

- ☐ Lt Gold - 165 yards (151 meters)
- ☐ Lt Yellow - 120 yards (110 meters)
- ☐ Yellow - 75 yards (68.5 meters)
- ☐ White - 20 yards (18.5 meters)
- ☐ Black - 15 yards (13.5 meters)
- ☐ Brown - 5 yards (4.5 meters)

Crochet Hook

- ☐ Size E (3.5 mm)

Additional Supplies

- ☐ 9½" (24 cm) Plastic canvas circle
- ☐ Polyester fiberfill
- ☐ Yarn needle

GAUGE INFORMATION

Gauge is **not** of great importance as long as your crochet fabric is very dense ***(see Gauge, page 43)***.

STAND

With Lt Gold, work Basic Stand, page 2.

RINGS

With Lt Yellow, work all 4 Basic Rings, page 5.

APPLIQUÉS

Hex

Rnd 1 (Right side)**:** With Brown, make an adjustable loop to form a ring; work 6 sc in ring; do **not** join, place a marker to indicate the beginning of the rnd.

Note: Mark Rnd 1 as **right** side.

Rnd 2: 2 Sc in each sc around: 12 sc.

Rnd 3: (Sc in next sc, 2 sc in next sc) around: 18 sc.

Rnd 4: (Sc in next 2 sc, 3 sc in next sc) around; slip st in next sc, finish off leaving a long end for sewing: 30 sc.

Using photo as a guide for placement and having **wrong** side of Hex against base of Stand, sew Hex in place.

Bee (Make 20)

With Yellow, ch 6; sc in second ch from hook, hdc in next ch, dc in next ch, hdc in next ch, 2 sc in last ch; working in free loops on opposite side of ch ***(Fig. 2, page 44)***, hdc in next ch, dc in next ch, hdc in next ch, sc in next ch; join with slip st to first sc, finish off leaving a long end for sewing.

Using photo as a guide:

- Sew 6 Bee appliqués evenly spaced around base of Stand.
- Sew 5 Bee appliqués evenly spaced around Bottom Ring.
- Sew 4 Bee appliqués evenly spaced around Second Ring.

- Sew 3 Bee appliqués evenly spaced around Third Ring.
- Sew 2 Bee appliqués evenly spaced around Top Ring.
- Using Black, add 4 stripes to each Bee appliqué using straight stitch ***(Fig. 5, page 45)***.
- Using Black, add a French knot eye to each Bee appliqué ***(Fig. 7, page 45)***.

Wing (Make 42)

Rnd 1 (Right side)**:** With White, make an adjustable loop to form a ring; work 6 sc in ring; join with slip st to first sc, finish off leaving a long end for sewing.

Sew two Wings to the top of each Bee appliqué, leaving the top of the Wings unsewn (you should have 2 Wings left to sew to 3-D Bee that follows).

3-D Bee

Rnd 1 (Right side)**:** With Yellow, make an adjustable loop to form a ring; work 6 sc in ring; do **not** join, place a marker to indicate the beginning of the rnd.

Rnd 2: 2 Sc in each sc around: 12 sc.

Rnd 3: Sc in each sc around changing to Black in last sc made ***(Fig. 3, page 44)***, drop Yellow.

Rnd 4: Sc in each sc around changing to Yellow in last sc made, drop Black.

Rnd 5: Sc in each sc around changing to Black in last sc made, drop Yellow.

Rnd 6: Sc in each sc around changing to Yellow in last sc made, cut Black.

Rnds 7 and 8: Sc in each sc around.

Stuff piece with polyester fiberfill.

Rnd 9: Sc2tog around; slip st in next sc, finish off leaving a long end for sewing.

Weave yarn end through the sts on the last rnd to close; secure end.

- Sew 2 remaining Wings to 3-D Bee.
- Using Black, add 2 French knot eyes.
- Sew 3-D Bee to top of Stand.

sprinkled Donuts

Finished Height: Approximately 6½" (16.5 cm)

EASY

SHOPPING LIST

Yarn (Medium Weight)

- ☐ Grey - 185 yards (169 meters)
- ☐ Beige - 100 yards (91.5 meters)
- ☐ Brown - 25 yards (23 meters)
- ☐ Pink - 30 yards (27.5 meters)
- ☐ Dk Brown - 25 yards (23 meters)
- ☐ Aqua - 25 yards (23 meters)
- ☐ White - 20 yards (18.5 meters)

Crochet Hook

- ☐ Size E (3.5 mm)

Additional Supplies

- ☐ 9½" (24 cm) Plastic canvas circle
- ☐ Safety pin
- ☐ Polyester fiberfill
- ☐ Embroidery floss (for Sprinkles) - Orange, Pink, Yellow, Aqua, Brown and White
- ☐ Tapestry needle
- ☐ Yarn needle

GAUGE INFORMATION

Gauge is **not** of great importance as long as your crochet fabric is very dense *(see Gauge, page 43)*.

STAND

With Grey, work Basic Stand, page 2, through Rnd 35; at end of Rnd 35, slip loop from hook onto safety pin: 35 sc.

With Grey, sew around Rnd 26 securing the top to the bottom through the canvas circle. This will prevent any fiberfill from going into the sides of the base and will keep the bottom flat to look like a plate.

Beginning with Rnd 36, complete same as Basic Stand.

Ruffle

Rnd 1: With **right** side of the bottom facing and working around the outside edge of the base (Rnd 16), join Grey with sc in any st ***(see Joining With Sc, page 44)***; sc in each st around; do **not** join, place a marker to indicate the beginning of the rnd.

Rnd 2: 2 Sc in each sc around; slip st in next sc, finish off.

RINGS

Bottom Ring

With Beige, work same as Basic Bottom Ring, page 5.

FROSTING

Rnd 1 (Right side)**:** With Pink, ch 42; being careful **not** to twist ch, sc in first ch to form a ring, sc in next 5 chs, 2 sc in next ch, (sc in next 6 chs, 2 sc in next ch) around; do **not** join, place a marker to indicate the beginning of the rnd: 48 sc.

Note: Mark Rnd 1 as **right** side.

Rnd 2: (Sc in next 7 sc, 2 sc in next sc) around: 54 sc.

Rnd 3: (Sc in next 8 sc, 2 sc in next sc) around: 60 sc.

Rnd 4: (Sc in next 9 sc, 2 sc in next sc) around: 66 sc.

Rnd 5: (Sc in next 10 sc, 2 sc in next sc) around: 72 sc.

Rnds 6 and 7: Sc in each sc around; at end of last rnd, slip st in next sc, finish off leaving a long end for sewing.

With tapestry needle and embroidery floss, add straight stitch sprinkles to frosting *(Fig. 5, page 45)*.

With long end, sew **wrong** side of Frosting to Ring.

Second Ring

With Beige, work same as Basic Second Ring.

FROSTING

Rnd 1 (Right side)**:** With Dk Brown, ch 36; being careful **not** to twist ch, sc in first ch to form a ring, sc in next 4 chs, 2 sc in next ch, (sc in next 5 chs, 2 sc in next ch) around; do **not** join, place a marker to indicate the beginning of the rnd: 42 sc.

Note: Mark Rnd 1 as **right** side.

Rnd 2: (Sc in next 6 sc, 2 sc in next sc) around: 48 sc.

Rnds 3-5: Work same as Bottom Ring Frosting, page 25, Rnds 2-4: 66 sc.

Beginning with Rnd 6, complete same as Bottom Ring Frosting.

Third Ring

With Beige, work same as Basic Third Ring.

FROSTING

Rnd 1 (Right side)**:** With Aqua, ch 30; being careful **not** to twist ch, sc in first ch to form a ring, sc in next 3 chs, 2 sc in next ch, (sc in next 4 chs, 2 sc in next ch) around; do **not** join, place a marker to indicate the beginning of the rnd: 36 sc.

Note: Mark Rnd 1 as **right** side.

Rnd 2: (Sc in next 5 sc, 2 sc in next sc) around: 42 sc.

Rnd 3: (Sc in next 6 sc, 2 sc in next sc) around: 48 sc.

Rnds 4 and 5: Work same as Bottom Ring Frosting Rnds 2 and 3: 60 sc.

Beginning with Rnd 6, complete same as Bottom Ring Frosting.

Top Ring

With Brown, work same as Basic Top Ring.

FROSTING

Rnd 1 (Right side)**:** With White, ch 24; being careful **not** to twist ch, sc in first ch to form a ring, sc in next 2 chs, 2 sc in next ch, (sc in next 3 chs, 2 sc in next ch) around; do **not** join, place a marker to indicate the beginning of the rnd: 30 sc.

Note: Mark Rnd 1 as **right** side.

Rnd 2: (Sc in next 4 sc, 2 sc in next sc) around: 36 sc.

Rnd 3: (Sc in next 5 sc, 2 sc in next sc) around: 42 sc.

Rnd 4: (Sc in next 6 sc, 2 sc in next sc) around: 48 sc.

Rnd 5: (Sc in next 7 sc, 2 sc in next sc) around: 54 sc.

Beginning with Rnd 6, complete same as Bottom Ring Frosting.

tower of Flowers

Finished Height: Approximately 8½" (21.5 cm)

EASY

SHOPPING LIST

Yarn (Medium Weight)

- ☐ Lime - 195 yards (178 meters)
- ☐ Yellow - 110 yards (101 meters)
- ☐ Orange - 105 yards (96 meters)
- ☐ Pink - 105 yards (96 meters)
- ☐ Aqua - 100 yards (91.5 meters)

Crochet Hook

- ☐ Size E (3.5 mm)

Additional Supplies

- ☐ 9½" (24 cm) Plastic canvas circle
- ☐ Polyester fiberfill
- ☐ Yarn needle

GAUGE INFORMATION

Gauge is **not** of great importance as long as your crochet fabric is very dense *(see Gauge, page 43)*.

STITCH GUIDE

TREBLE CROCHET
(abbreviated tr)
YO twice, insert hook in st indicated, YO and pull up a loop (4 loops on hook), (YO and draw through 2 loops on hook) 3 times.

STAND

With Lime, work Basic Stand, page 2.

Leaf (Make 8)

With Lime and leaving a long end for sewing, ch 10; sc in second ch from hook, hdc in next 2 chs, dc in next 2 chs, tr in next 3 chs, 4 tr in last ch; working in free loops on opposite side of ch ***(Fig. 2, page 44)***, tr in next 3 chs, dc in next 2 chs, hdc in next 2 chs, sc in next ch; join with slip st to first sc, finish off.

Sew one Leaf to each of the 8 bottom edges of the Stand.

RINGS

Bottom Ring

With Orange, work same as Basic Bottom Ring, page 5.

PETAL (Make 6)

Rnd 1 (Right side)**:** With Pink, make an adjustable loop to form a ring; work 6 sc in ring; do **not** join, place a marker to indicate the beginning of the rnd.

Note: Mark Rnd 1 as **right** side.

Rnd 2: 2 Sc in each sc around: 12 sc.

Rnd 3: (Sc in next sc, 2 sc in next sc) around: 18 sc.

Rnd 4: (Sc in next 2 sc, 2 sc in next sc) around: 24 sc.

Rnd 5: (Sc in next 3 sc, 2 sc in next sc) around: 30 sc.

Rnd 6: (Sc in next 4 sc, 2 sc in next sc) around: 36 sc.

Rnds 7-9: Sc in each sc around; at end of Rnd 9, finish off leaving a long end for sewing.

Fold petals in half and sew evenly spaced around Bottom Ring.

Second Ring

With Aqua, work same as Basic Second Ring.

PETAL (Make 6)

With Yellow, work same as Bottom Ring Petal.

Fold petals in half and sew evenly spaced around Second Ring.

Third Ring

With Yellow, work same as Basic Third Ring.

PETAL (Make 5)
With Orange, work same as Bottom Ring Petal.

Fold petals in half and sew evenly spaced around Third Ring.

Top Ring

With Pink, work same as Basic Top Ring.

PETAL (Make 5)
With Aqua, work same as Bottom Ring Petal.

Fold petals in half and sew evenly spaced around Top Ring.

all hands on Deck

Finished Height: Approximately 10¼" (26 cm)

EASY

SHOPPING LIST

Yarn (Medium Weight) MEDIUM 4

- ☐ Lilac - 265 yards (242 meters)
- ☐ Teal - 140 yards (128 meters)
- ☐ Pink - 120 yards (110 meters)
- ☐ Rose - 45 yards (41 meters)
- ☐ White - 5 yards (4.5 meters)

Crochet Hook

- ☐ Size E (3.5 mm)

Additional Supplies

- ☐ Polyester fiberfill
- ☐ Black embroidery floss (for features)
- ☐ Tapestry needle
- ☐ Yarn needle

GAUGE INFORMATION

Gauge is **not** of great importance as long as your crochet fabric is very dense ***(see Gauge, page 43)***.

STITCH GUIDE

TREBLE CROCHET
(abbreviated tr)

YO twice, insert hook in st indicated, YO and pull up a loop (4 loops on hook), (YO and draw through 2 loops on hook) 3 times.

STAND

With Lilac, work Basic Stand, page 2, through Rnd 16: 120 sc.

Next 4 Rnds: Sc in each sc around.

Beginning with Rnd 17, complete same as Basic Stand.

Tentacles

LONG (Make 4)

Row 1: With Lilac and leaving a long end for sewing, ch 45; sc in second ch from hook and in next 14 chs, hdc in next 10 chs, dc in next 10 chs, tr in last 9 chs: 44 sts.

Row 2: Ch 4 **(counts as first tr)**, turn; tr in next 8 tr, dc in next 10 dc, hdc in next 10 hdc, sc in next 5 sc, slip st in next sc, leave remaining 9 sc unworked; finish off leaving a long end.

SHORT (Make 4)

Row 1: With Lilac and leaving a long end for sewing, ch 35; sc in second ch from hook and in next 9 chs, hdc in next 10 chs, dc in next 10 chs, tr in last 4 chs: 34 sts.

Row 2: Ch 4 **(counts as first tr)**, turn; tr in next 3 tr, dc in next 10 dc, hdc in next 10 hdc, sc in next 5 sc, slip st in next sc, leave remaining 4 sc unworked; finish off leaving a long end for sewing.

SUCKER (Make 36)

Rnd 1 (Right side)**:** With Rose, make an adjustable loop to form a ring; work 6 sc in ring; join with slip st to first sc, finish off leaving a long end for sewing.

Note: Mark Rnd 1 as **right** side.

With **wrong** side of Sucker against Tentacle, sew 4 Suckers to each short Tentacle and 5 Suckers to each long Tentacle.

Using second long end on each Tentacle, sew a long running stitch along the edge ***(Fig. A)*** and pull to gather, shape as desired; knot and secure end.

Fig. A

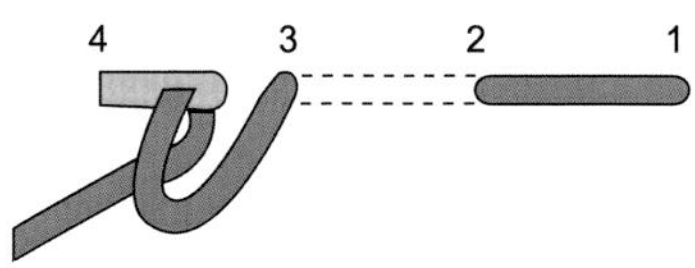

With first long end, sew Tentacles evenly around the bottom of the Stand, alternating between Long and Short.

Features

EYE (Make 2)

Rnd 1 (Right side)**:** With White, make an adjustable loop to form a ring; work 6 sc in ring; do **not** join, place a marker to indicate the beginning of the rnd.

Note: Mark Rnd 1 as **right** side.

Rnd 2: 2 Sc in each sc around; slip st in next sc, finish off leaving a long end for sewing.

CHEEK (Make 2)

Rnd 1 (Right side)**:** With Rose, make an adjustable loop to form a ring; work 6 sc in ring; join with slip st to first sc, finish off leaving a long end for sewing.

Note: Mark Rnd 1 as **right** side.

Using photo as a guide for placement:

- Sew Eyes to base approximately 5 sc apart.
- With Black floss and referring to Embroidery Stitches, page 45, add pupils, eyelashes, and wide smile.
- Using long end, sew Cheeks in place.

RINGS

Bottom Ring

With Teal, work same as Basic Bottom Ring, page 5.

TRIANGLE (Make 10)

Row 1 (Right side)**:** With Teal, ch 16; sc in second ch from hook and in each ch across: 15 sc.

Note: Mark Row 1 as **right** side.

Rows 2-7: Ch 1, turn; beginning in first sc, sc2tog, sc in each sc across to last 2 sc, sc2tog: 3 sc.

Row 8: Ch 1, turn; sc in first sc, sc2tog: 2 sc.

Row 9: Ch 1, turn; sc in first sc, slip st in last st, finish off.

Holding 2 Triangles with **wrong** sides together, sew end of rows together, leaving the beginning ch edge free.

Place the open edges evenly around ring, and sew in place, stuffing with polyester fiberfill before closing.

Second Ring

With Pink, work same as Basic Second Ring.

TRIANGLE (Make 10)
Row 1 (Right side)**:** With Pink, ch 14; sc in second ch from hook and in each ch across: 13 sc.

Note: Mark Row 1 as **right** side.

Rows 2-6: Ch 1, turn; beginning in first sc, sc2tog, sc in each sc across to last 2 sc, sc2tog: 3 sc.

Beginning with Row 8, complete same as Bottom Ring Triangle.

Third Ring

With Teal, work same as Basic Third Ring.

TRIANGLE (Make 10)
Row 1 (Right side)**:** With Teal, ch 12; sc in second ch from hook and in each ch across: 11 sc.

Note: Mark Row 1 as **right** side.

Rows 2-5: Ch 1, turn; beginning in first sc, sc2tog, sc in each sc across to last 2 sc, sc2tog: 3 sc.

Beginning with Row 8, complete same as Bottom Ring Triangle.

Top Ring

With Pink, work same as Basic Top Ring.

TRIANGLE (Make 10)
Row 1 (Right side)**:** With Pink, ch 12; sc in second ch from hook and in each ch across: 11 sc.

Note: Mark Row 1 as **right** side.

Rows 2-5: Ch 1, turn; beginning in first sc, sc2tog, sc in each sc across to last 2 sc, sc2tog: 3 sc.

Beginning with Row 8, complete same as Bottom Ring Triangle.

Using photo as a guide for placement, add a smiling face and eyes onto each starfish ring using Black embroidery floss.

sunny Rainbow

Finished Height: Approximately 10½" (26.5 cm)

EASY

SHOPPING LIST

Yarn (Medium Weight)

- ☐ Blue - 150 yards (137 meters)
- ☐ Green - 40 yards (36.5 meters)
- ☐ Yellow - 40 yards (36.5 meters)
- ☐ Orange - 35 yards (32 meters)
- ☐ Red - 25 yards (23 meters)
- ☐ White - 15 yards (13.5 meters)

Crochet Hook

- ☐ Size E (3.5 mm)

Additional Supplies

- ☐ 9½" (24 cm) Plastic canvas circle
- ☐ Polyester fiberfill
- ☐ Yarn needle

GAUGE INFORMATION

Gauge is **not** of great importance as long as your crochet fabric is very dense ***(see Gauge, page 43)***.

STAND

With Blue, work Basic Stand, page 2.

Cloud (Make 4)

With White, ch 6; 4 dc in second ch from hook, slip st in next ch, 3 hdc in next ch, slip st in next ch, 4 dc in last ch; working in free loops on opposite side of ch ***(Fig. 2, page 44)***, slip st in next 2 chs, 4 dc in next ch, slip st in next ch; join with slip st to first dc, finish off leaving a long end for sewing.

Sew the Clouds evenly spaced around the base.

Sun Topper

Rnd 1 (Right side)**:** With Yellow, make an adjustable loop to form a ring; work 6 sc in ring; do **not** join, place a marker to indicate the beginning of the rnd.

Note: Mark Rnd 1 as **right** side.

Rnd 2: 2 Sc in each sc around: 12 sc.

Stuff piece with polyester fiberfill.

Rnds 3 and 4: Sc in each sc around.

Rnd 5: Sc2tog around; slip st in next sc, finish off leaving a long end for sewing: 6 sc.

Weave yarn end through sts on the last rnd to close ***(Fig. 4, page 44)***; secure end.

RAYS

Working in sts around side of sun (Rnd 3), join Orange with sc in any sc ***(see Joining With Sc, page 44)***; ch 4, (sc in next sc, ch 4) around; join with slip st to first sc, finish off leaving a long end for sewing.

Sew Sun Topper to top of the Stand.

RINGS

Bottom Ring

With Green, work same as Basic Bottom Ring, page 5.

Second Ring

With Yellow, work same as Basic Second Ring.

Third Ring

With Orange, work same as Basic Third Ring.

Top Ring

With Red, work same as Basic Top Ring.

General Instructions

ABBREVIATIONS

ch(s)	chain(s)
cm	centimeters
dc	double crochet(s)
hdc	half double crochet(s)
mm	millimeters
Rnd(s)	Round(s)
sc	single crochet(s)
sc2tog	single crochet 2 together
st(s)	stitch(es)
tr	treble crochet(s)
YO	yarn over

SYMBOLS & TERMS

( ) or **[ ]** — work enclosed instructions **as many** times as specified by the number immediately following **or** contains explanatory remarks.

colon (:) — the number(s) given at the end of a row or round denote(s) the number of stitches or spaces you should have on that row or round.

CROCHET TERMINOLOGY		
UNITED STATES		INTERNATIONAL
slip stitch (slip st)	=	single crochet (sc)
single crochet (sc)	=	double crochet (dc)
half double crochet (hdc)	=	half treble crochet (htr)
double crochet (dc)	=	treble crochet (tr)
treble crochet (tr)	=	double treble crochet (dtr)
double treble crochet (dtr)	=	triple treble crochet (ttr)
triple treble crochet (tr tr)	=	quadruple treble crochet (qtr)
skip	=	miss

Yarn Weight Symbol & Names	LACE 0	SUPER FINE 1	FINE 2	LIGHT 3	MEDIUM 4	BULKY 5	SUPER BULKY 6	JUMBO 7
Type of Yarns in Category	Fingering, size 10 crochet thread	Sock, Fingering, Baby	Sport, Baby	DK, Light Worsted	Worsted, Afghan, Aran	Chunky, Craft, Rug	Super Bulky, Roving	Jumbo, Roving
Crochet Gauge* Ranges in Single Crochet to 4" (10 cm)	32-42 sts**	21-32 sts	16-20 sts	12-17 sts	11-14 sts	8-11 sts	6-9 sts	5 sts and fewer
Advised Hook Size Range	Steel*** 6 to 8, Regular hook B-1	B-1 to E-4	E-4 to 7	7 to I-9	I-9 to K-10½	K-10½ to M/N-13	M/N-13 to Q	Q and larger

*GUIDELINES ONLY: The chart above reflects the most commonly used gauges and hook sizes for specific yarn categories.

** Lace weight yarns are usually crocheted with larger hooks to create lacy openwork patterns. Accordingly, a gauge range is difficult to determine. Always follow the gauge stated in your pattern.

*** Steel crochet hooks are sized differently from regular hooks–the higher the number, the smaller the hook, which is the reverse of regular hook sizing.

GAUGE

Gauge is not of great importance; your project may be a little larger or smaller without changing the overall effect. It is best to use a small hook and tight single crochet stitches. The holes between the stitches need to be very small, making your crochet fabric dense. The stuffing should not stretch the fabric or show through the stitches. Use the size hook needed to achieve a tight gauge.

ADJUSTABLE LOOP

Wind the yarn around two fingers to form a ring ***(Fig. 1a)***, slide the yarn off your fingers and grasp the strands at the top of the ring ***(Fig. 1b)***. Insert the hook from **front** to **back** into the ring, pull up a loop, YO and draw through the loop on hook to lock the ring ***(Fig. 1c)***. Working around **both** strands, work stitches in the ring as specified, then pull the yarn end to close ***(Fig. 1d)***.

Fig. 1a

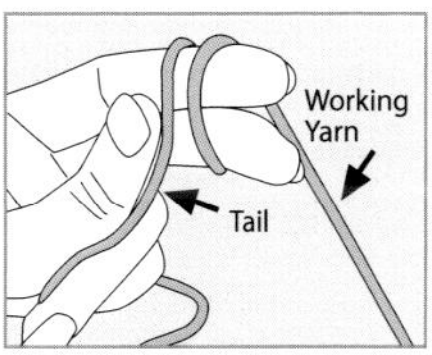

Fig. 1b

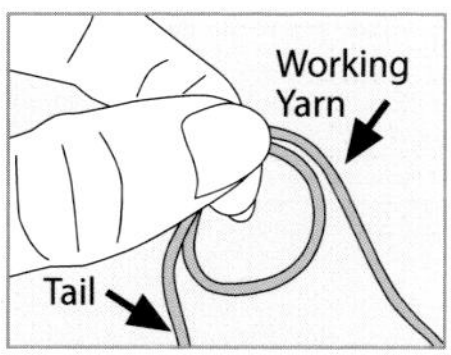

Fig. 1c

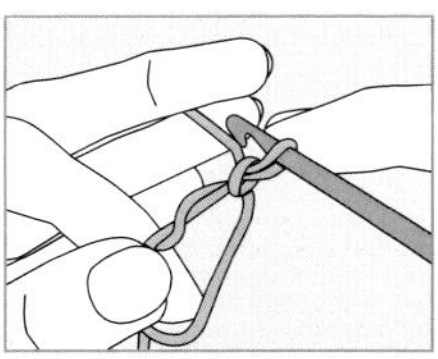

Fig. 1d

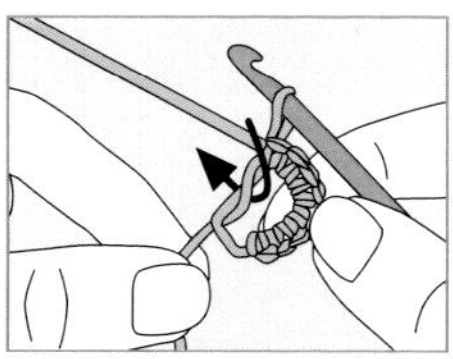

BEGINNER	Projects for first-time crocheters using basic stitches. Minimal shaping.
EASY	Projects using yarn with basic stitches, repetitive stitch patterns, simple color changes, and simple shaping and finishing.
INTERMEDIATE	Projects using a variety of techniques, such as basic lace patterns or color patterns, mid-level shaping and finishing.
EXPERIENCED	Projects with intricate stitch patterns, techniques and dimension, such as non-repeating patterns, multi-color techniques, fine threads, small hooks, detailed shaping and refined finishing.

CROCHET HOOKS	
U.S.	Metric mm
B-1	2.25
C-2	2.75
D-3	3.25
E-4	3.5
F-5	3.75
G-6	4
7	4.5
H-8	5
I-9	5.5
J-10	6
K-10½	6.5
L-11	8
M/N-13	9
N/P-15	10
P/Q	15
Q	16
S	19

MARKERS

Markers are used to help distinguish the beginning of each round being worked. Place a 2" (5 cm) scrap piece of yarn before the first stitch of each round, moving the marker after each round is complete.

JOINING WITH SC

When instructed to join with a sc, begin with a slip knot on the hook. Insert hook in stitch or space indicated, YO and pull up a loop, YO and draw through both loops on hook.

FREE LOOPS OF A CHAIN

When instructed to work in free loops of a chain, work in loop indicated by arrow *(Fig. 2)*.

Fig. 2

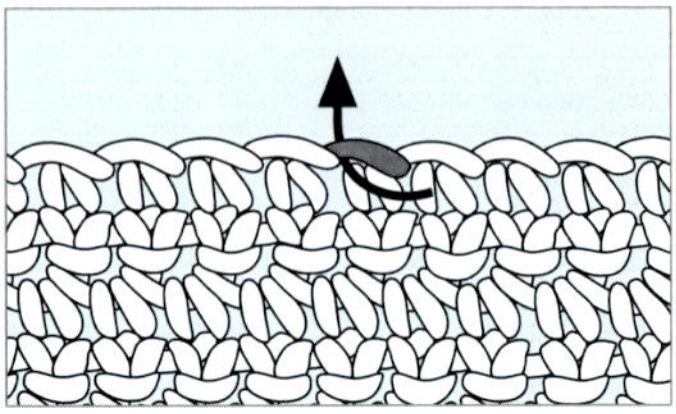

CHANGING COLORS

Insert hook in stitch indicated, YO and pull up a loop, drop yarn, with new yarn *(Fig. 3)*, YO and draw through both loops on hook. Do **not** cut yarn until indicated.

Fig. 3

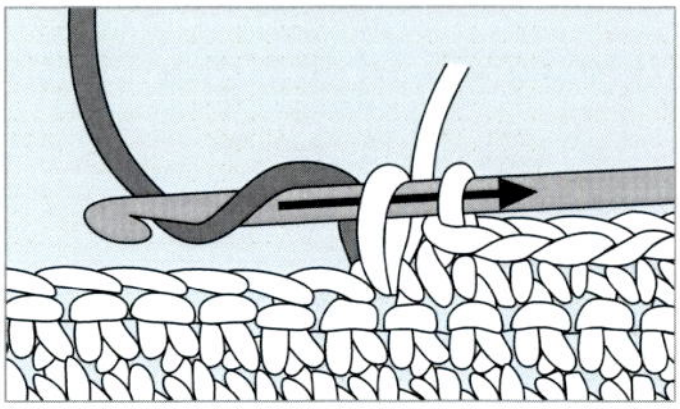

WEAVE THRU STITCHES

Weave yarn end through the stitches *(Fig. 4)* and gather to close.

Fig. 4

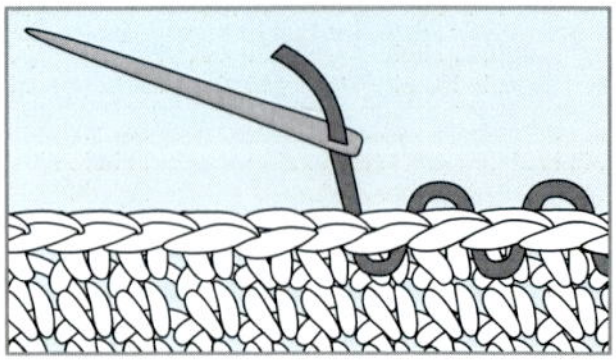

EMBROIDERY STITCHES

Straight Stitch

Straight stitch is just what the name implies, a single, straight stitch. Come up at 1 and go down at 2 ***(Fig. 5)***.

Fig. 5

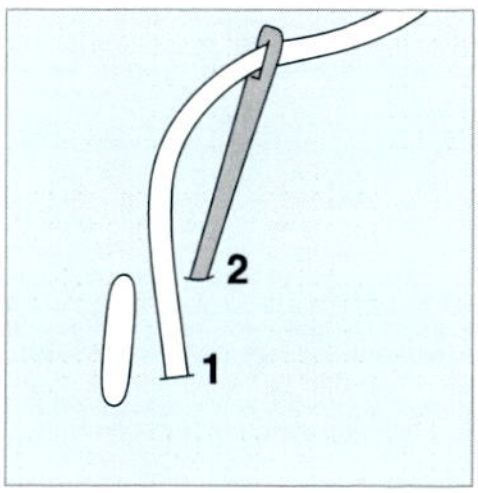

Satin Stitch

Satin stitch is a series of straight stitches worked side-by-side that touch but do not overlap ***(Fig. 6a)*** or come out of and go into the same stitch ***(Fig. 6b)***. Come up at odd numbers and go down at even numbers.

Fig. 6a

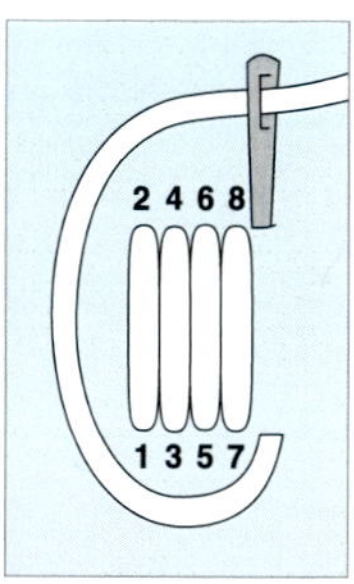

Fig. 6b

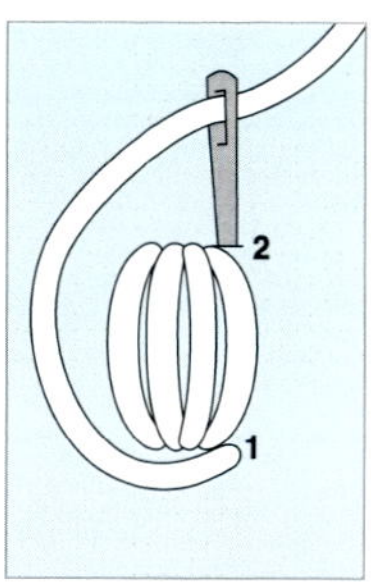

French Knot

Bring the needle up at 1. Wrap yarn around the needle the desired number of times and insert needle at 2, holding end of yarn with non-stitching fingers ***(Fig. 7)***.

Tighten knot; then pull needle through, holding yarn until it must be released.

Fig. 7

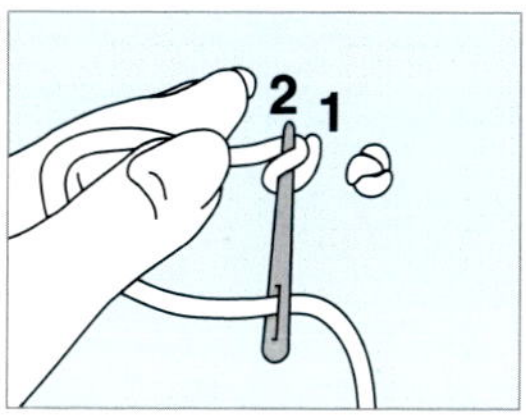

Yarn Information

The Stacks in this book were made using medium weight yarn. Any brand of medium weight yarn may be used. It is best to refer to the yardage/meters when determining how many skeins or balls to purchase. Remember to arrive at the finished size, it is the GAUGE/TENSION that is important, not the brand of yarn.

For your convenience, listed below are the yarn used to create our photography models. Because yarn manufacturers make frequent changes in their product lines, you may sometimes find it necessary to use a substitute yarn or to search for the discontinued product at alternate suppliers (locally or online).

SO CUTE SAFARI!

Red Heart® Super Saver®

Green - #0631 Lt Sage

Red Heart® Soft®

Teal - #9520 Seafoam

Blue - #9820 Mid Blue

Dk Brown - #9344 Chocolate

Lt Grey - #9440 Lt Grey Heather

Caron® Simply Soft®

Gold - #0008 Autumn Maize

Lt Blue - #9709 Lt Country Blue

Tan - #9703 Bone

Orange - #9765 Pumpkin

White - #9701 White

Red Heart® With Love®

Dk Yellow - #1207 Cornsilk

IT'S THE BEES!

Red Heart® With Love®

Lt Gold - #1207 Cornsilk

Brown - #1970 Taupe

Red Heart® Super Saver®

Lt Yellow - #0235 Lemon

Yellow - #0324 Bright Yellow

White - #0311 White

Black - #0312 Black

SPRINKLED DONUTS

Red Heart® With Love®

Grey - #1401 Pewter

Lion Brand® Vanna's Choice®

Beige - #123 Beige

Brown - #124 Toffee

Caron® Simply Soft®

Pink - #0015 Strawberry

Dk Brown - #9750 Chocolate

Aqua - #9608 Blue Mint

White - #9701 White

TOWER OF FLOWERS

Red Heart® Super Saver®

Lime - #0672 Spring Green

Yellow - #0324 Bright Yellow

Orange - #0254 Pumpkin

Red Heart® With Love®

Pink - #1704 Bubblegum

Aqua - #1969 Wintergreen

ALL HANDS ON DECK

Red Heart® Soft®

Lilac - #9528 Lilac

Teal - #9870 Deep Sea

Rose - #9770 Rose Blush

Caron® Simply Soft®

Pink - #0015 Strawberry

White - #9701 White

SUNNY RAINBOW

Red Heart® With Love®

Blue - #1803 Blue Hawaii

Yellow - #1201 Daffodil

Orange - #1971 Tigerlily

Red Heart® Super Saver®

Green - #0624 Tea Leaf

Red - #0319 Cherry Red

White - #0311 White

Production Team: Instructional/Technical Editor - Linda A. Daley; Senior Graphic Artist - Lora Puls; Photo Stylist - Lori Wenger; and Photographer - Jason Masters.

meet Tamara Ramsey

Tamara Ramsey enjoys crocheting simple and colorful soft toys for kids of all ages.

"I've been creating soft toys for my own children as well as my friends and family for the past 13 years," she says. Since 2011, she also has been selling her toys and patterns through her website at ostuffandfluff.etsy.com. *Baby's Buddy Amigurumi* was her first book with Leisure Arts.

"I taught myself how to make amigurumi toys from free patterns I found online. After I had made a few, I saw how the basic shapes were made and realized I could alter these shapes to make my own animals."

Bunnies and dolls are her favorite projects. "I tend to find a yarn color I like and then build a pattern around it. My kids help me a lot, too! They give me ideas for new animals, and they help me decide what details should be added."

When it comes to crocheting amigurumi, she encourages people to just have fun. "If your row gets off by a stitch and then does not work out right, it's OK!" she says. "Crochet is very forgiving, and you can easily add another stitch or decrease a stitch and keep going. It's supposed to be fun, not stressful. Being off by a stitch or two will not change the look of your pattern. I know the child who cuddles your toy will never notice! The important thing is to enjoy creating something and have fun."

Tamara works on her crochet projects in the evenings, after home-schooling her three children during the day. She and her husband recently finished Bible college and began work as pastors of their first church.

Made in U.S.A.